Budgeting Your Money

by Stuart Schwartz and Craig Conley

Consultant:
Robert J. Miller, Ph.D.
Professor of Special Education
Mankato State University

CAPSTONE
HIGH/LOW BOOKS
an imprint of Capstone Press
Mankato, Minnesota

Capstone High/Low Books are published by Capstone Press
818 North Willow Street • Mankato, MN 56001
http://www.capstone-press.com

Library of Congress Cataloging-in-Publication Data
Schwartz, Stuart, 1945–
        Budgeting your money/by Stuart Schwartz and Craig Conley.
        p. cm.—(Life skills)
        Includes bibliographical references and index.
        Summary: Explains how to budget money, discussing income, savings, fixed
and variable expenses, living expenses, and economizing.
        ISBN 0-7368-0044-1
        1. Finance, Personal—Juvenile literature. 2. Budgets, Personal—Juvenile
literature. [1. Budgets, Personal. 2. Finance, Personal.] I. Conley, Craig, 1965–
II. Title. III. Series: Schwartz, Stuart, 1945–   Life skills.
HG179.S338   1999
640'.42—dc21
                                                                                98-35111
                                                                                    CIP
                                                                                    AC

Editorial Credits
Christy Steele, editor; James Franklin, cover designer and illustrator; Michelle L.
   Norstad, photo researcher

Photo credits
All photographs by Barb Stitzer Photography

Table of Contents

Chapter 1

Budgets

People sometimes spend more money than they earn. They then do not have enough money for necessary spending such as bills. In these cases, people may owe money to other people. The amount of money people owe is a debt. Many people make budgets to help them stay out of debt.

Budgets help people decide the best way to spend the money they earn. People use budgets to plan necessary spending and to save money.

People need supplies to create budgets. People use notebooks, pencils, and calculators. Some people buy special budget books. Other people use computer programs to create budgets. People should always keep their budget supplies in one place. This helps people find the budget information they need.

It is important to keep track of expenses. People list all their expenses on their budgets. People should save important receipts. These pieces of paper show that money, goods, or services have been received.

Many people make budgets to help them stay out of debt.

Chapter 2

Advantages of Budgeting

Budgets help people plan the best use of their money. People can decide what items they can afford to buy when they use a budget.

Budgets also help people save money for the future. People put aside money to buy important items. For example, people save money to pay for cars, vacations, or furniture. Many people save money for the years after they retire.

Budgets help people see how much money they waste on things they do not need. For example, people might spend too much money on clothing. They may eat out too often or at too many expensive restaurants.

People who keep budgets can find out how and where they spend their money. Budgets help people learn to use their money wisely and stay out of debt.

Budgets help people see how much money they waste buying things they do not need.

Chapter 3

Income

Income is the total amount of money a person makes or receives. People may receive income from many places. For example, they may receive income from jobs or as gifts. People also might do additional work such as mowing lawns for extra money. People must include all sources of income on their budgets.

People should add the amounts of money received after they list all their income sources. This amount is their total income. The total income is the amount available to spend and save.

People should write down their incomes each week, each month, and each year. Then they can see how much money they have at different times.

People must write down their incomes on their budgets.

Chapter 4

Fixed Expenses

Fixed expenses are bills people must pay regularly. The amount of a fixed expense stays the same each month. Rent is a fixed expense because people pay the same rent every month. Car payments and bank loan payments are fixed expenses too.

People should make a list of their yearly fixed expenses. They must add up all the amounts on that list to find the total.

Next, people should divide the total by 12. This is the amount of money people must set aside each month. They need this much money to pay for fixed expenses.

For example, someone has to pay for car insurance two times each year. This person should set aside money each month for the insurance. The person will then have enough money to pay the insurance bill.

People must make a list of their expenses.

Chapter 5

Living Expenses

Living expenses are harder to plan for than fixed expenses. People must pay for living expenses each month. But the amount they pay for living expenses changes from month to month. The cost of these expenses depends on changing prices. Food, clothes, telephone service, and gas for cars are some living expenses.

People must list their living expenses. They should guess the amount they usually spend each month on each living expense. For example, people must buy food. They should list how much they usually spend on food each month. Then they should add all their living expenses to see how much money they need each month.

People sometimes spend too much on living expenses before they pay their fixed expenses. Budgets help people balance their spending between fixed expenses and living expenses.

Food, clothing, entertainment, and gas for cars are some living expenses.

Chapter 6

Itemizing

People should make a list of their most important expenses. They should rank these expenses in order of their importance. The most important item would be number one. This is itemizing. A budget must include fixed expenses and living expenses. It should also include items people want to buy.

Fixed expenses are the most important expenses. They should be ranked highest. Living expenses are next in order of importance. Entertainment expenses are the least important.

People may not make enough money to pay for all the items on their lists. Then they must only buy the more important items. They should save money to buy the items that are lower on their itemized lists.

People should check their itemized lists every day. The list will remind them to spend their money wisely.

People itemize by making a list of expenses that are most important to them.

Chapter 7

Variable Expenses

Variable expenses are unexpected expenses. Car repairs and medical emergencies are examples of variable expenses.

It is hard to budget for variable expenses. But people need to make sure they have money to pay for unexpected expenses. People should put some money aside each month for this purpose.

People who do not budget for variable expenses often do not have enough money to pay for emergencies. They might have to use money they need for other important expenses. People then might run out of money. They might go into debt.

People must decide how much money to budget for variable expenses. People should add their variable expenses for the past year. Then they should divide that amount by 12. This gives people an idea of how much they need to set aside every month.

Variable expenses are unexpected expenses such as car repairs.

Chapter 8

Saving Money

People can create savings plans in their budgets. They can save to buy items such as cars and houses.

People should decide how much they can save each month. First, they need to subtract fixed expenses, living expenses, and variable expenses from their incomes. They should see if they have any money left. If they do, this money is discretionary income. People must decide how much of their discretionary income they want to save. Then they should write down that amount in their budgets.

People may have expensive items ranked low on their itemized lists. They may not have enough money to buy these items. Budgets show people how long they must save before they can buy these items. For example, a person may want to take a trip that costs $1,000. This person might save $100 each month. It will take this person 10 months to save the money for the trip.

Budgets help people create savings plans.

Chapter 9

Discretionary Income

People can spend discretionary income as they choose. People must decide how to use their discretionary income. Itemized lists help people spend discretionary income wisely.

People must decide which items they want and which items they really need. For example, a person may need to make car repairs. But the person also may want to take a vacation. People should buy the things they need before the things they want.

People may have to wait to buy everything on their itemized lists. They may also have to save part of their discretionary income for more expensive items.

A budget shows people how much they can spend on items they want. People must spend only their discretionary income on these items.

People can spend discretionary income as they choose.

Chapter 10

Keeping a Budget

People must plan their budgets carefully. They should follow the budgets they create and keep them up to date.

People must make sure they list all their living expenses, fixed expenses, and variable expenses. Many people create a heading in their budgets for each type of expense.

People write lists of specific expenses under each heading. Some listings under fixed expenses may be housing and car payments. Some listings under living expenses may be food and electricity. Listings under variable expenses may be gifts and personal expenses such as haircuts. People may add listings as they keep track of expenses.

Calendars make it easier for people to follow budgets. Many people write reminders on their calendars. Reminders help them remember when to pay their bills. Companies often charge extra money when people pay bills late. Late charges add to people's expenses.

Calendars make it easier for people to follow budgets.

Chapter 11

Keeping Track of Expenses

At first, people may find it difficult to keep track of expenses. But people can learn to write down all their expenses in their budgets.

People should save all their receipts. They can then add the amounts of the receipts. The total amount should be the same as the amount they wrote in their budgets. Receipts help people make sure they are listing expenses correctly.

Another good way to stay within a budget is to put money in a bank. People should take money out of their bank only for necessary items. They should take out only the amounts they have budgeted. People should never take out more money than they need. People should not spend money without planning ahead.

People should save all their receipts.

Chapter 12

Economizing

People often learn to economize when they follow a budget. To economize means to cut down on spending in order to save money. People who economize have more discretionary income.

People can economize in many ways. They can cut coupons out of newspapers or buy goods that are on sale. People might cook at home instead of eating at restaurants. They may buy used items instead of new items.

Careful records will show people what their greatest expenses are. People should examine these expenses to see where they can economize. For example, a person may see charges on a phone bill for a 60-minute long-distance call. The person can economize by limiting long-distance calls to 20 minutes.

Economizing helps people follow their budgets. People who economize have more money to pay bills and to save.

People economize by buying goods that are on sale.

Words to Know

budget (BUHJ-it)—a plan for spending and saving money

discretionary income (diss-KRE-shuh-nair-ee IN-kuhm)—money that remains after subtracting fixed expenses, living expenses, and variable expenses from income

economize (i-KON-uh-mize)—to cut down on spending to save money

fixed expense (FIKST ek-SPENSS)—a bill a person has to pay regularly; the amount of the bill stays the same.

income (IN-kuhm)—the total amount of money a person makes or receives

itemize (EYE-tuh-mize)—to make a list of expenses and rate the importance of each item

receipt (ri-SEET)—a piece of paper that shows the amount paid for goods or services

variable expense (VAIR-ee-uh-buhl ek-SPENSS)—an unexpected expense

To Learn More

Berg, Adriane G. and Arthur Berg Bochner.
*The Totally Awesome Money Book for Kids
(and Their Parents).* New York: Newmarket
Press, 1993.

Guthrie, Donna and Jan Stiles. *Real World
Math: Money, Credit, and Other Numbers in
Your Life.* Brookfield, Conn.: Millbrook Press,
1997.

Moose, Christina. *Budgeting.* Vero Beach,
Fla.: Rourke Publications, 1997.

Moose, Christina. *Debt.* Vero Beach, Fla.:
Rourke Publications, 1997.

Phillips, Jan. *Whole Numbers and Money.*
Syracuse, N.Y.: New Readers Press, 1995.

Useful Addresses

American Consumer Credit Counseling, Inc.
24 Crescent Street
Waltham, MA 02154

Civil Service Cooperative Credit Society
400 Albert Street
Ottawa, ON K1R 5B2
Canada

Consumer Credit Counseling Service
4600 Gulf Freeway, Suite 500
Houston, TX 77023-3551

J. W. Charles Securities, Inc.
599 Lexington Avenue, 22nd Floor
New York, NY 10022

Internet Sites

CCCS Budgeting in Six Easy Steps
http://www.cccsdc.org/6steps.html

The Dollar Stretcher
http://www.stretcher.com

Household Budget Management
http://lonestar.texas.net/~budget

Kids' Money
http://pages.prodigy.com/kidsmoney/index.htm

Money Management International
http://www.moneymanagementbymail.org/

Index